Penguin Books
Posts

Neville Gabie was born in Johannesburg, South Africa in 1959. He moved to England as a young teenager in the 1970s. He works predominantly as a sculptor, having studied at the Royal College of Art, London, though photography has always formed a considerable part of his practice. He has exhibited his work extensively in South Africa and the UK and is included in a number of collections, including the Arts Council Collection.

   This, his first published book, brings together his two passions of art and football. Neville Gabie is a Liverpool fan of long standing.

The distance between the posts is 7.32 m (8 yards) and the distance from the lower edge of the crossbar to the ground is 2.44 m (8 feet).

Both goalposts and the crossbar have the same width and depth which do not exceed 12cm (5 inches). The goal lines are the same width as that of the goalposts and crossbar.

Posts
Neville Gabie

PENGUIN BOOKS

PENGUIN BOOKS

Published by the Penguin Group
Penguin Books Ltd, 27 Wrights Lane, London W8 5TZ, England
Penguin Putnam Inc., 375 Hudson Street, New York, New York 10014, USA
Penguin Books Australia Ltd, Ringwood, Victoria, Australia
Penguin Books Canada Ltd, 10 Alcorn Avenue, Toronto, Ontario, Canada M4V 3B2
Penguin Books (NZ) Ltd, Private Bag 102902, NSMC, Auckland, New Zealand

Penguin Books Ltd, Registered Offices: Harmondsworth, Middlesex, England

First published in Penguin Books 1999
10 9 8 7 6 5 4 3 2 1

Typeset in Franklin Gothic Condensed in QuarkXPress™ 3.32
Colour reproduction by Dot Gradations Ltd, Essex
Printed in England by Jarrold Book Printing Ltd, Norfolk

A CIP catalogue record is available from the British Library

Cover photographs
Front: Masel bel Abbes, Tunisia
Back: Crowlas, Cornwall, England (top), Priory Fields, Tewkesbury, England (middle),
Glenpark Street, Belfast, Northern Ireland (bottom)
Front flap: Boisen Ardres, France

Foreword

In the past couple of years or so, I have regularly fended off the 'question': no, they are not all white, measured and set within manicured lawns. Goalposts, whilst being universally recognizable, are as unique and individual as the people and places where the game is played. These images elucidate that point more eloquently than words. The more interesting question is: what triggered the obsession with photographing goalposts?

More by accident than design, its beginnings are to be found in the landscapes of South Africa. Whilst making sculpture in these rural locations, I became increasingly aware of wooden goalposts, standing out like beacons of human endeavour in often vast, empty spaces. I was fascinated by the sheer inventiveness of their construction. Within the narrow perimeters of creating a structure out of three 'sticks' (two vertical, one horizontal), the imaginative use of material and the variety of solutions to that always difficult problem of joining two bits of wood together, lies the basis of sculpture.

As the project developed, I began to see how the posts mirrored their environment. Where there was no wood to hand, stones, string, metal, chalk or paint could be used. And without a field in which to play, a garage door, a street corner or a car park become reasonable substitutes. With minimal means, these goalposts eloquently expressed much of what I was trying to achieve through making sculpture. They encapsulate our dreams and fantasies, and the uniqueness of 'place', in a language which is universally understood.

Many thousands of miles later, my opinion has not altered. Rather, as is often the case in pursuing an idea, I have had other insights. Standing in a bare earth field strewn with brick and stone, wedged between the railway line and shanty town, I met a man who used to watch a very young Maradona play there. So for some the back yard is really where it all begins.

Soccer is the 'global' game, and no matter where you are in the world, goalposts are so familiar a part of the landscape they go unnoticed. They exist like streetlights or telegraph poles, necessary but unconsidered. Symbol of the game, most goalposts are white and upright ... but some aren't.

Even with a project as single-minded as this one, I owe a huge debt of thanks to a great many people. To Charles Frewin and Dan Jacobson, without whose encouragement and time this book would never have happened. To David Jones for his unswerving loyalty, technical expertise and hours spent in the car. To Daniel Peyrou, the best of South American guides, and to my brother Graham for all his time. To Tony Lacey, Liz Halsall, Phil Treble and all the staff at Penguin for taking a chance on so unusual a book.

Finally I would like to dedicate this book to Joan, Freya, Tobias and William.

'Goalposts and crossbars must be made of wood, metal or other approved material.'

FIFA rule book

Zrig, Tunisia →

to roll
to crease
to fold
to store
to bend
to shorten
to twist
to dapple
to crumple
to shave
to tear
to chip
to split
to cut
to sever
to drop
to remove
to simplify
to differ
to disarrange
to open
to mix
to splash
to knot
to spill
to droop
to flow
to curve

to lift
to inlay
to impress
to fire
to flood
to smear
to rotate
to swirl
to support
to hook
to suspend
to spread
to hang
to collect
of tension
of gravity
of entropy
of nature
of grouping
of layering
of felting
to grasp
to tighten
to bundle
to heap
to gather
to scatter
to arrange

to repair
to discard
to pair
to distribute
to surfeit
to complement
to enclose
to surround
to encircle
to hide
to cover
to wrap
to dig
to tie
to bind
to weave
to join
to match
to laminate
to bond
to hinge
to mark
to expand
to dilute
to light
to modulate
to distill
of waves

of electromagnetic
of inertia
of ionization
of polarization
of refraction
of simultaneity
of tides
of reflection
of equilibrium
of symmetry
of friction
to stretch
to bounce
to erase
to spray
to systematize
to refer
to force
of mapping
of location
of context
of time
of carbonization
to continue

Richard Serra,
a personal manifesto for making sculpture

1
2
3

1 Le Kef, Tunisia
2 Saidan, Tunisia
3 Greylingstad, South Africa

Debewielkie, Poland

Francistown, Botswana

KM 169 Ciudad, Del Este, Paraguay

Crowlas, Cornwall, England

Retiro Railway Station, Buenos Aires, Argentina

'Nets may be attached to the goals and the ground behind the goal, provided that they are properly supported and do not interfere with the goalkeeper.' FIFA rule book

Callanais, Isle of Lewis, Scotland

1st de Mayo, Paraguay

Asunción, Paraguay

Kilmonivaig, Fort William, Scotland

South View Rise, Cheltenham, England

Middleburg, South Africa

Maria Auxiliadora, Paraguay

Cedar Street, Glasgow, Scotland

'Their shape may be square, rectangular, round or elliptical and they must not be dangerous to players.'

FIFA rule book

Parkhead, Glasgow, Scotland

Rinmore Drive, Londonderry, Northern Ireland

'If the crossbar becomes displaced or broken, play is stopped until it has been repaired or replaced in position. If a repair is not possible, the match is abandoned.' **FIFA rule book**

'And you good yeomen,
Whose limbs were made in
England, show us here
The mettle of your pasture.'

William Shakespeare, *Henry V*

Clutha Street, Ibrox, Glasgow

Berkeley, Gloucestershire, England

Longfellow Street, Bootle, England

Suwałki, Poland

Calle Araoz de Lamadrid, Buenos Aires, Argentina

Acton Street, Shankhill Road, Belfast, Northern Ireland

Haffouz, Tunisia

Newry, Northern Ireland

Calle Vespucio, Buenos Aires, Argentina

Botafogo Bay, Rio de Janeiro, Brazil

Cerro Porten, Asunción, Paraguay

FIFA rule book **'The goalposts**

Pont d'Ardres, France

Dachra, Tunisia

and crossbars must be white.'

'Serious sport has nothing to do with fair play. It is bound up with hatred, jealousy, boastfulness, disregard of all the rules and sadistic pleasure in witnessing violence: in other words it is war minus the shooting.' George Orwell

Shakespeare Street, Bootle, England

'The decisions of the referee regarding facts connected with play are final. This may include: a decision that the condition of the field of play or its surrounds or that the weather conditions are such as to allow or not to allow a match to take place.' **FIFA rule book**

57° 52' N / 06° 57' W

57° 46' N / 06° 56' W

Seilebost, Harris, Outer Hebrides
Pitch: flat, with coarse coastal grass and the odd hole (thanks to rabbits) making play difficult. Island location facing on to the Atlantic, this field catches the worst of the winter storms. Wind here is a constant problem.

Lingarabay, Harris, Outer Hebrides
Pitch: narrow and uneven, located on a small area of grass between rocks. Very wet underfoot. Island location, exposed to the full brunt of the weather, which can be miserable even during the summer months.

← **Priory Fields, Tewkesbury, England**

51° 44' N / 02° 09' W

56° 36' N / 24° 12' E

Eastcombe, England
Pitch: exposed on the top of a hill, this field catches the brunt of the winter weather. It is usually wet and muddy underfoot and subject to strong winds.

Iecava, Poland
Pitch: located within an orchard, the ground is uneven with ruts, craters and long grass. During the long winter months it is also usually frozen hard. Exposed to extreme winter weather, much of it in darkness.

56° 53' N / 24° 08' E

56° 51' N / 24° 21' E

Riga, Latvia
**Pitch: flat with a good covering of grass. Winter here starts early,
with snow being a constant feature throughout those months.
Lack of daylight adds to the impossibility of playing during
winter.**

Salaspils, Latvia
**Pitch: flat with a good covering of grass. Located within yards of
a Holocaust site. Winter here starts early, with snow being a
constant feature throughout those months. Lack of daylight
adds to the impossibility of playing during winter.**

Bergville, South Africa
Pitch: well maintained with grass cut. Although usually dry
during winter months, being at a high altitude, there can be
unpredictable and heavy snowfalls. Spectacular location in the
Drakensburg foothills.

Mont aux Scource, South Africa
Pitch: flat with grass, short though slightly uneven. Five
thousand feet above sea-level and weather can be unpredictable,
though winter months are usually dry. The surroundings are
spectacular.

23° 13' S / 44° 43' W

34° 36' S / 58° 27' W

Parati, Brazil
Pitch: coastal sand which can be soft or heavy depending on
weather. Located in one of the first Portuguese ports to be settled
on this coast, the area has changed little. Usually hot, though
subject to tropical storms.

Calle Vespucio / Calle California, Buenos Aires, Argentina
Pitch: uneven, bare earth with many hazards. Beware of stones,
metal and glass, which can be found strewn over the field and
make playing difficult.

22° 35' S / 42° 42' W

23° 13' S / 44° 46' W

Japuiba, Brazil
Pitch: bare earth in a small narrow clearing. The surface is uneven, rutted and not helped by tropical rains, which are frequent and heavy.

Serra da Bocaina, Brazil
Pitch: flat, with grass, though worn in the goalmouths and centre of the field. Very hot, tropical conditions, with high humidity and heavy tropical rains which seem to stay on the surface.

57° 17' N / 05° 37' W

53° 24' N / 06° 16' W

Balmacara, Lochalsh, Scotland
Pitch: flat, well-maintained grass pitch in a spectacular location. Exposed to the elements, and during the winter months can be very cold. Heavy snowfalls are a regular feature through winter.

Ballymun, Ireland
Pitch: flat grass, though extreme caution should be taken when playing on this field. Needles, used syringes and a range of other litter are to be found on and around the playing area. Often wet, but generally a moderate climate.

Feriana, Tunisia
Pitch: sloping, uneven and worn bare by constant use. Stony surface, some of the stones quite large. No pitch markings and improvised posts. Hot and uncompromising conditions.

Fos sur Mer, France
Pitch: flat Astra turf with a covering of fine sand. Coastal Mediterranean climate which is generally pleasant.

27° 12' S / 49° 09' W

43° 42' N / 07° 13' E

Ribeirão do Ouro, Brazil
Pitch: flat, bare earth, hard underfoot. Located in a small clearing amongst trees on a hillside, memorable in particular for the birdsong and forest smells. Temperature is tropical.

Route de Turin / Ave les Ecoles, Nice, France
Pitch: earth and loose gravel in an enclosed yard. Some glass to be found on pitch. Mediterranean temperatures generally very pleasant.

50° 55' N / 00° 59' E

42° 46' N / 11° 38' E

Dungeness, England
Pitch: shingle beach with large stones making the surface almost impossible to play on. Being coastal, the weather can range from pleasantly warm to extremely foggy and windy. An unusual location, with some unique beach gardens near by.

Selvena, Italy
Pitch: hard, uneven surface, a mix of earth, dry grass and stone. Mountainous region with little respite from the sun for most of the year. Winters can be wet but are invariably short.

35° 47' N / 10° 59' E

24° 42' S / 23° 00' E

Helya Hotel, Monastir, Tunisia
Pitch: uneven beach sand and long, dry grass. Located yards from the sea. Temperatures here are pleasant during the winter and extremely hot during summer months.

Sossusvlei, South Africa
Pitch: flat, loose sandy surface, but ground very hard. Beware of stones, some large, found across the field. Being in the desert, sandstorms are common. Temperatures are also extreme with the air being tangibly dry.

33° 42' N / 08° 58' E

28° 26' S / 17° 32' E

Kebilli, Tunisia
Pitch: flat, baked hard, though rutted by recent rains. Much used and generally in good condition. Mild during winter months, though often extremely hot during summer.

Sesfontein, Namibia
Pitch: flat, bare earth, baked hard, though the top surface is loose underfoot. Stones, wood and fragments of metal and glass found on the pitch. Hot and dry for most of the year, though when it rains it is usually heavy.

'Sweet day,
so cool,
so calm,
so bright'

George Herbert

Pułtusk, Poland

Barra da Tijuca, Brazil

'Every time he played here he

S. R. Vincente Aridraia and S. R. Paul José Martinez, Argentinos Juniors, on Maradona

Villa Fiorito, Buenos Aires, Argentina, birthplace of Maradona

left his soul on the pitch.'

'Among artists, there are those who risk standing out and those who don't.' Eric Cantona

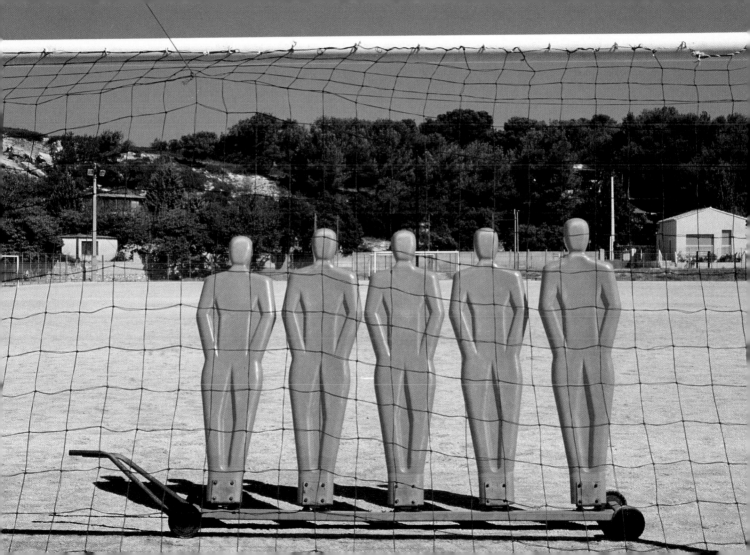

Cruzeiro, Brazil

Clogger Head, Ireland

Khorixas, Namibia

Tres Corações, Brazil, birthplace of Pele

'Brazilians learn to kick as soon as they learn to stand up; walking comes later.' Pele

'If you wanted George, you looked in that field, and he'd be there with a ball.'

Dickie Best, George's father

Rue Vincent Scotto, Arles, France

Dungeness, England

Avenida Itaybaite, Asunción, Paraguay

'The border between soccer and politics is vague.'

Quoted by Ryszard Kapuscinski

KINALLEN COURT

Ormeau Road, Belfast, Northern Ireland

I.R.A U.T.P

RELEASE ALL POW's NOW

SAOIRSE

'We must keep watching from the depths of a definitive silence, for the definitive event.' Jean Baudrillard

Marins, Pompiers, Marseilles, France

Scarasta, Harris, Outer Hebrides

'No kind of commercial advertising, whether real or virtual, is permitted on the field of play'

FIFA rule book

St Martin de Crau, France   Mareth, Tunisia   Liverpool, England

'A few I understand, in writing home, have styled my efforts as "wanderings". The very word contains a

Mtynska, Poland

San Andrés de la Barca, Spain

Hilman Street, Antrim Road, Belfast

lie coiled like a serpent in its bosom. It means travelling without an object, or uselessly.'

David Livingstone, Missionary and Explorer, 1853